Measuring Aggressive Behavior Perceptions

Published by Spines
ISBN 979-8-89691-628-4

Measuring Aggressive Behavior Perceptions

Dr. Tammarra R. Jones

MEASURING AGGRESSIVE BEHAVIOR PERCEPTIONS
Tammarra R. Jones
Submitted in Partial Fulfillment of Requirements for the
Degree of Doctor of Psychology

Acknowledgments

This work is dedicated to Reverend Ruth Stubbs Jones and the late Mr. Nathaniel Ray Jones, my parents. It is also dedicated to Learning Disabilities Teacher-Consultant, Ms. Kumesia Williams and Program Manager, Ms. Marchette Johnson. This work was enabled in part by Mr. William Stubbs and Mrs. Bonnie Davis Stubbs, my maternal grandparents. The Creator and the ancestors have blessed this work and it was completed with thanks to the tradition of the ancient Egyptian principle Maat.

Special thanks is extended to the committee, Dr. Yuma Tomes, Dr. George McCloskey, and Dr. Cheryl Thompson. You all were my light and I am very grateful for your wonderful guidance.

ABSTRACT

Poverty, which can be classified as perpetual, and resource mismanagement are among causes for negative outcomes in central city, public education settings. Learned helplessness is the focal point among the results of the creation of this circumstance of perpetual poverty (*the great insult*). The manifestation of learned helplessness is unique in this instance and can be remedied with Learned Hopefulness. The purpose of this study is to teach children (both classified special education and general education students) in central city and surrounding community schools about their African history which is rich and about which they know little. Group drumming is culturally relevant, and supports the value of collectivism present in many Eastern- based cultures. Reflection and self-disclosure have been considered activities that help to reduce stress.

The Child Behavior Checklist Aggression Problem Scale (CBCL) was used to measure learner aggressive disruptions to the learning session. After the testing period, self-esteem improved and aggressiveness was reduced. This was a quantitative study using the, paired samples, repeated measures approach. In order to determine if aggressive behaviors and disruptive impulses were reduced as per Child Behavior Checklist for Ages 6-18 based Aggressive Behaviors and Disruptive Impulses survey, scores were completed by parents and teachers of the 32 fifth grade, 10-year-old boys.

A dependent t-test was conducted in each of the twenty areas determined to reflect physical, social/emotional, internalizing and externalizing behaviors. This study provided good evidence of the benefits of group drumming to make schooling a viable resource for children. Low cost and accessible, drumming can be free style or can follow ancient rhythms from almost every continent.

CONTENTS

CHAPTER 1

MEASURING AGGRESSIVE BEHAVIOR PERCEPTIONS

INTRODUCTION

Africans and their descendants are among the many different people who have made substantial contributions to the development and civilization of humanity. Too often, history has proven that these contributions are negated due to the global perspectives that position people of color in something less than what is reserved for others in human hierarchy. The works of some, not unlike the authors of texts like The Bell Curve, assert genetic distinctions among human beings that significantly impact intelligence and adaptation. These philosophies have been vastly accepted and perpetuated in many arenas that require human interaction.

People of African heritage can often be easily identified by color. Even though race is a socio-political concept that has more meaning in the U.S. than in other places, that American, contemporary, global culture suggests norms for the rest of the world. When the world history discussion about contributions omits or diminishes Black people in America and their ancestors, that has significant implications for Black skinned people everywhere.

In late 1994, the publication of The Bell Curve made the word "eugenics" familiar in the American lexicon again. The research quoted in the book is drawn overwhelmingly from members of the American Eugenics Society and other eugenics groups. The conclusion of the book is that men are not equal, and that the Declaration of Independence is badly worded. Eugenicists strongly espoused racial supremacy and "purity," particularly of the "Aryan" race. Eugenicists hoped to purify the bloodlines and improve the race by encouraging the "fit" to reproduce and the "unfit" to restrict their reproduction. They sought to contain the "inferior" races through segregation, sterilization, birth control and abortion. Eugenics is the study of methods to improve the human race by controlling reproduction. The word was first used in 1883 by Francis Galton, a cousin of Charles Darwin. Galton believed that the proper evolution of the human race was thwarted by philanthropic outreach to the poor, when such efforts encouraged them to bear more children. Charity upset the mechanism of natural selection, according to Galton and others. Galton wanted eugenics to develop from a science, to a policy and finally into a religion.

The general distrust of dominant group institutions is justified if one examines health care, criminal justice, and policing structures. However, in education, children of African descent are often ignored and underestimated to the point of exclusion. The fact that black children are, in many ways, devalued makes the need to assert oneself in many classrooms, understandable. What is viewed as aggressive behavior from children in the classroom, by those who teach them, may be a child's imperfect attempt to be included and recognized as a willing learner.

The eugenics espousers of the twentieth century, including early Planned Parenthood leadership, encouraged the sterilization of African women here and on the African continent as well as throughout the diaspora. The objective was to control poverty, and disease by restricting the reproductive liberty of Africans. Instead of acknowledging the greed and lack of fairness and equity that caused poverty and inequality, the victims of irresponsible policies and institutions were blamed for the problems others caused and perpetuated. Some health professionals still encourage African women to limit the children that they have based on their assumption that economic disempowerment will compromise the lives of those children. The act of being born, for some children, is considered an aggressive act (Randall 1996). What has presented itself in schools is the phenomenon of the School to Prison Pipeline. The School to Prison Pipeline assumes that children are best prepared to serve society as imprisoned, virtual slave laborers who must be managed. These residual effects of the eugenics movement provide tangible, horrific realities that need to be reversed.

Children's art and literature, folklore, the study of languages, science, economics, law, and education all presume the exclusion of the African contribution in contemporary societies. The contributions of the African Diaspora are countless, and under perfect circumstances would render world-wide acclaim. However, global structures have systematically imposed hundreds of years of intense brutality, and demoralizing tactics, such as attempting to erase the contributions of people of color out of world history, by omitting particular data from texts and curricula. These methods have weakened the self-concept of men and women of color. Imagine the impact that it has on children of color. How does this translate into the school system?

Children of color in urban schools are often regarded as

psychologically unhealthy and are exploited by adult systems more often than their white counterparts (Fenning 2007). Nonetheless, children of color are resilient, often tapping into their innate resources defying obstacles that are set before them. The challenge as educators, exceeds beyond practical teaching techniques. Instead it is imperative to investigate coping and overcoming strategies that are organic to this culture of students and their families. This is a copious task that is expected to yield tried, true, and tested measures that will produce children of color with a healthy and productive response to their environments.

Self-Concept

In the influential work *The Warrior Method: A Parents' Guide to Rearing Healthy Black Boys*, (Winbush 2002) argues that ancient Africans from western and south-western regions of the continent had their own way of dealing with building self-concept. When a community member did not affirm healthy behaviors, he or she was encircled at the community square by elders, peers, and family members. The person was verbally and sometimes ritualistically reminded of all of the "good" contributions made to the community that impacted others. Because of this positive reinforcement, the person became overwhelmed with instances of his or her own positive behavior. The elders offered additional counseling to the person, thus correcting the injury done as a result of the offensive behaviors. This is an authentic and exemplary execution of functional positive behavior support. Not only was the offensive behavior acknowledged and corrected, the entire community modeled an appropriate and corrective response to their young.

According to Alexander (2012) in her book, *The New Jim*

Crow," by targeting black men through the War on Drugs and decimating communities of color, the U.S. criminal justice system functions as a contemporary system of racial control—relegating millions to a permanent second-class status—even as it formally adheres to the principle of colorblindness."(Pg.49) The ancient African process of reconciliation and forgiveness stands in stark contrast to the contemporary function of the Prison Industrial Complex enterprise that is prevalent in the United States. It seems that the main goal of this system is merchandising and the practice of arresting and incarcerating people of color in mass numbers, hence using the labor of these people to create profit for commercial entities in both public and private sectors. An educator's concern in this matter is the result of the School to Prison Pipeline phenomenon- that is the systematic exclusion of children of color from the public school experience (with all of its legal safeguards). With this in mind, children of color are generally directed to earning sources outside of the legal realm.

On the opposite end of the legal system, many years ago when African-American students entered law school they were asked to name five individual or collective African-ethnic groups. They were unable to complete this simple task. One might question their own unawareness as it related to their heritage and self-concept. Why is it that mounting ignorance about Africa and her systems are obscured and denied? Can drumming and learning about your history increase self-aware-ness, self-concept, and self- pride, thus improving your perfor-mance in school?

STATEMENT OF THE PROBLEM

Maafa or the Swahili term *Maafa* ("Great Disaster") in English, was introduced by Mariamba Ani' in her book "Let the Circle

Be Unbroken: The Implications of African Spirituality in the Diaspora". It is derived from a Swahili term for "disaster, terrible occurrence or great tragedy", Some Afrocentric scholars prefer the term *Maafa* to *African Holocaust*, because they believe that indigenous African terminology more truly confers the events. The term *Maafa* may serve much the same cultural, psychological purpose for Africans as the idea of the *Holocaust* serves to name the culturally distinct Jewish experience of genocide under German Nazism.

Other arguments in favor of *Maafa* rather than *African Holocaust*, emphasize that the denial of the validity of the African people's humanity is an unparalleled, centuries-long phenomenon: "The Maafa is a continual, constant, complete, and total system of human negation and nullification." (Ani 1994). Convict Leasing, Jim Crow policies, Segregation, modern-day aggressions, systematic brutality from law enforcement, combined with underdevelopment provide the continuum to help analyze poverty and the larger systems that encourage and enable perpetual poverty in the modern-era. It is unreasonable to think that after more than two centuries of relentless oppression and ruthless violence that slavery has simply ended, without leaving any traces of psychological impact on future generations. The effects of Maafa seem to have extended even in the development of the fetus in the womb.

One has only to examine the speeches and letters orated and written by Willie Lynch (1712) to slaveholders. Lynch was deliberate and clear in his desire for generational control over enslaved Africans. The criticism that some doubt the authenticity of Lynch's speeches and letters seems irrelevant when one examines the behaviors of slaveholders. In the West Indies and North America where Lynch was a dominant presence,

Africans were systematically dehumanized and terrorized. The climate of terror, constant separation of loved ones, and intense poverty had disastrous effects on enslaved families.

In many instances, children of African heritage cannot look to the body of knowledge in most curricula and find themselves as objects and subjects of their learning. In addition, the instructors they find in classrooms are often the youngest, least experienced, and least effective among teachers. African contributions in qualitatively meaningful ways have been excluded from the cannon. Authors including Molefi Asante and Ivan Van Sertima, along with clinicians and researchers like Amos Wilson and Na'im Akbar have worked without mainstream acknowledgement. When we re-insert the realities of Africa both contemporary and traditional for all children, but especially for children of color, into the body of knowledge, they can find connection and purpose.

The ACA program is designed to accomplish this objective to the extent that is possible. Can learning about oneself before and during Maafa help in developing the skills needed to change or at least positively impact that condition? The drum is the center of the community in that it is also symbolic of the heartbeat or a symptom of the life force that connects all living things. For too long African heritage children were required to see themselves as something other than the heir to a scientific and literate past. That omission of the true nature of the African's contribution needs to be corrected.

The Multi-Generational Injury: Learned Helplessness.

In her thought-provoking work *Post-Traumatic Slave Syndrome*, Degruy (2005) defines Post Traumatic Slave Syndrome (PTSS) as a condition that exists as a consequence of multi-generational oppression of Africans and their descendants. This described set of conditions includes Learned Helplessness, or the belief that any attempt to positively impact one's condition will be overwhelmingly negated. This realization is sometimes imprinted via generational exchange and the genetic memory of centuries of chattel slavery. This experience was then followed by "institutional racism" which continues to perpetuate injury. According to Degruy (2005), key patterns of behavior reflective of PTSS include vacant esteem that is evidenced by a facial expression analysis, a marked propensity for anger and violence, racist socialization, antipathy for members of one's own cultural group and cultural dissonance.

THE NEED FOR THE STUDY

In extensive research conducted by Niane (1965) about the history of The Old Malian Empire which comprised a large part of West Africa, the people of these areas developed their lives and incorporated music and dance into all aspects of it. There are even dances and songs that retell Maafa from the perspectives of Africans who remained on the continent, as well as those who were removed. However, for every occasion there was at least a dance and song.

Learning about African cultures before the Triangular Slave Trade and specifically focusing on the celebrations of life can serve as a reawakening of curiosity about learning, as a result helping in developing self-regulation skills. These celebrations included the focus on physically and emotionally handicapped people within the community. These efforts teach resilience in very practical and simplistic ways. The drumming experience can produce benefits for the individual or as part of a drum circle or group. The child drummer can express him or herself more efficiently because of the introduced experience of self-awareness. This leads to better communication with peers and cooperative play. Therefore, it transcends into the greater community and contributes to continuous positive development over time.

PURPOSE OF THE STUDY

Wilson (1978), in his text, *The Developmental Psychology of the Black Child*, asserts that a careful examination of scientific, historical and socio-psychological evidence helps us to see critical differences among Black children and other children. DeGruy, (2005) has considered some of the information presented by Wilson (1978), and has emphasized that those who are descendants of enslaved people suffer from Post Traumatic Slave Syndrome. The purpose of this study is to teach children "learned hopefulness" and other resilience skills in the context of their rich African history. Traditional drumming, dancing and singing of the West-African region, and learning about the geography of cultures of other African regions will be the substance of the African Cultural Arts (ACA) program. It is expected that improvements in self-esteem and self-concept will follow as a result of participation in this program and will motivate students to participate more effectively in the educative process. By allowing students to be the subjects of their study and seeing themselves reflected in positive ways in the substances of learning novice material, they will begin to recognize the value in examining their own heritage.

When people come to expect that they cannot control important aspects of their lives, the results may be more crippling than we would presume. The central idea in Learned Helplessness theory is the notion that all animals (including humans) are able to learn that those stimuli that reinforce are uncontrollable (Seligman, 1992). The theory of learned help-lessness postulates that this may lead to a maladaptive behavior pattern, resulting in a lowering of performance in ordinary activities and feelings of powerlessness. The expectation of uncontrollability is formed through cognitive processes of perception and attribution. It seems also that developmental experiences play a significant role in establishing and rein-forcing such tendencies (Emmanuel, 1991-1992). The trau-matic experiences of *Maafa* (both direct and vicarious), to children are particularly damaging, and are devastating to the entire group and may signal the genocide of a people.

Summary

Poverty, which can be classified as perpetual, and resource mismanagement are among causes for negative outcomes in central city, public education settings. The characteristics for the establishment of perpetual poverty are met in the lives of many African-descended students, including those who are trained in international settings. Those conditions and charac-teristics can be isolated and identified most easily in American contexts during the Great Enslavement, but also can be traced through convict leasing, sharecropping, peonage, Jim/Jane Crow, legal segregation, de facto segregation, the struggle for human rights, and periods of contemporary injury and back-lash. Learned helplessness is the focal point among the results of the creation of this circumstance of perpetual poverty (*the great insult*). The manifestation of learned helplessness is unique in this instance and can be remedied with Learned Hopefulness. The purpose of this study is to teach children (both classified special education and general education students) in central city and surrounding community schools about their African history which is rich and about which they know little. We hope to teach the traditional drumming, dancing and singing of various African regions. We also hope to teach the geography and culture of those regions in order to encourage children and adolescents to engage in the educative process in more meaningful ways.

CHAPTER 2

———————

LITERATURE REVIEW

INTRODUCTION

In the seminal autobiographical work *Up from Slavery*, Washington (1901) details memories of his life as a child in Maafa and revelations as he lived and worked as an adult during Reconstruction and post-Reconstruction. Washington's desire was to help create a solid foundation in the country for development among "the hands, the heads and the hearts" of formerly enslaved Africans in North America (Washington 1901). Washington's holistic perspective is echoed in the educative settings of ancient Egypt, settings in Timbuktu, the ancient civilizations of Greece and Rome and those of the modern age.

Educational development can have good results in national conditions of stability and equity. Washington produced great results during some of the worst national conditions for people of African descent living in America at any time. It may have been that since Washington knew the hardships of surviving slavery and its transitions in North America, he considered the hand first to provide the economic promise of consistency in access to meaningful work, so that formerly enslaved Africans could meet their material needs. Countering the challenge of the theories of diminished humanity of Africans, Washington may have realized and savored the "freedom" one enjoys when one can inform herself with information that will improve her life and perhaps the lives of her descendants. He knew that the dominant group was afraid of African empower-ment. In order to facilitate continued cooperation with benefactors, Washington may have emphasized certain advantages in intellectual development for African students, but in a less emphatic way than he addressed the development of the hands.

Finally, Washington knew that survival, however meager the resources available, was essential to growth for a people, who hoped to coexist with their former masters. The survival of African Americans was precarious and Washington worked to stabilize the entire group by producing scholars from slaves who could determine and execute the best lives possible for themselves and their people. It is important to be aware of the ways in which dysfunctional responses to racial oppression get in the way of black people being able to organize, collaborate, network, mentor and support one another. Black-Greek organizations are international mentoring groups that have to function under a cloak of secrecy and mystery, ostensibly because the development of the scholarly, African Self was a threat to the system of racial oppression. The Handbook of Mental Health and Mental Disorder among Black Americans, edited by Ruiz (1990), provides good resources for understanding component processes to African American psychological health and liberation.

Self-Conceptualizations

In the summary of the chapter entitled "Practical Strategies for Coping with the Impact of Racial Oppression", Landrum-Brown (1990) asserts that optimally functioning black (people) are not driven by dysfunctional responses to internalized racial oppression. They are not limited by the conceptual restraints of an imposed, anti-self, worldview. They are not alienated from parts of themselves or from their African heritage and culture. They are not limited to their awareness of available internal and external resources; and they can use these resources for adaptive, healthy, and developing psychological functioning (Ruiz 1990). Landrum-Brown includes several terms that will help to define and explain Self Concept as conceptualized for this work. Among them are racism, internalized racial oppression or self- hatred or self-loathing behaviors, conceptual imposition and incarceration, split-self syndrome, self-knowledge, world-view analysis and self-view analysis, conceptual liberation, and emotional liberation.

Self-Analysis

In the Self-Analysis process, it is important to discern value-laden connotations in one's self-descriptions. One must give oneself permission to tell the truth, without personal condemnation. It is important to pay attention to one's feelings about the self, so that one can be empowered with the most accurate information. Landrum-Brown suggests making a personal strengths and weaknesses list by the individual and two significant others. After comparisons of the lists is done, any omitted items can be added. The process includes questioning, reflection and acknowledgement. Internal resources to make improvements in areas of weakness can be more easily used if they have been accurately identified.

Self-Knowledge

"Self-Knowledge is the basis of all true knowledge" (James 1976). When individuals pay attention to the verbal and nonverbal interactions in relationships they may be able to learn much about the parts of themselves they might overlook or deny. Growth through self-exploration can be a difficult process. It is important that one provide remedy and treatment, if necessary to reflect, understand and intervene effectively in maladaptive thoughts, feelings, attitudes and behaviors.

Effects of Racism

"Racism is an infection of the belief system, a mental illness with the following symptoms: 1) perceptual distortion, 2) denial of reality, 3) delusions of grandeur, 4) projections of blame (to the victim) 5) phobic reactions to differences" (Hilliard, 1978). Racism is determined by the individual who has the power to impose his biases and prejudices on others as a group. Individual behavior, which may be crude, vile and immoral is racist when it is applied by a member of the dominant group in an oppressive environment.

Internalized Racial Oppression

Internalized racial oppression (Landrum & Batts, 1985) is a psychological response exhibited by racially different individuals to the negative messages inherent in racism. It involves the acceptance of racially oppressive messages communicated by those who are racially different. Generally, this phenomenon is expressed in several ways. The first is system beating which involves "getting over on" or acting out against the system. The next is blaming the system which involves taking little or no responsibility for one's actions. The third is total avoidance of whites and the Euro-American system, evidenced as anti-white separatism. Next is the denial of blackness and African heritage, including distrusting blacks, devaluing African culture and overvaluing and accepting whites as superior and; Finally, denial of the political signifi-cance of race and racism, which may include a host of expres-sions including learned helplessness (Landrum-Brown 1990). Learned helplessness, the belief that one is powerless and doomed in the face of one's oppressor is a residual impact of the eugenics perspective and has very little basis in fact except as a self-fulfilling prophesy.

CONCEPTUAL IMPOSITION AND INCARCERATION

When one is conceptually incarcerated, (Nobles, 1978) one is able to see what is real only through an imposed and culturally different perspective or worldview. The world view, establishes a personal structure to relate to the world and define reality. Perceptions regarding nature, the self, other people, institutions, objects, the universe and God consciousness are all formed or conceptualized according to the world view. It can be influ-enced by strong feelings, memories, assumptions, expectations, past experiences, attitudes, values and beliefs. Conceptual incarceration can have as its nexus, punishment by the domi-nant group for deviating from imposed Anglo Saxon Protestant standards for perceiving reality, using language, and making life-style choices; or some person's lacking the capacity to conceptualize anything other than an anti-self-perspective. It, (Conceptual Incarceration), is broader than internalized racial oppression because it encompasses a wider range of variables other than race.

SPLIT-SELF SYNDROME

The Split-Self Syndrome is a result of accepting a polarized, hierarchical manner of "either/or" "all or none" thinking. It includes accepting negative racial messages that may result from internalized racial oppression or conceptual incarceration. For African Americans who are black, living in a society that devalues blackness and African-ness, the splitting, appears to be the result of having internalized negative messages about their racial differences. In order to feel accepted and valued, one is compelled with a desire to disown one's very self.

CONCEPTUAL LIBERATION

The healing process for African Americans living in a racially oppressive society requires letting go of any distorted and false, anti-self, anti-African messages that they have internalized. Conceptual liberation involves restructuring personal perceptions and thoughts in ways that will counter distorted and false beliefs, assumptions and messages. Many times individuals can reshape self-perspectives and self-perceptions and make whole a fragmented world view. Problems with assertiveness, stress, depression, and destructive expressions of anger can be treated by this process.

EMOTIONAL LIBERATION

Liberation is the release from oppression. Emotional liberation not only requires release from the emotional dependence on others for self -definition, it also requires that one become active in determining what is best for oneself and working to create inner and outer environments that support the full emancipated self. When one has learned to choose feelings expression by noting appropriate and constructive ways to vent, one has become emotional liberated. When one can transform one's way of being in the world to be more harmonious with others and with nature, according to the belief system one subscribes to, then one will be spiritually liberated. When one comes to accept and love those aspect of the physical self that cannot be changed, one has become physically liberated. Conceptual liberation includes the process of monitoring and reconstructing one's world view and way of being that is more psychologically self-affirming and freeing.

What Landrum-Brown has omitted is painfully obvious. Individuals must have control over the resources in their immediate and extended environments to produce and distribute the wealth they generate in order to determine their economic and financial well-being. The inner processes are critical for the development of the Self. External conditions have to be hospitable at least, in order for liberation of any individuals can be realized.

Disruptive Behaviors

Disruptive behavior is any behavior that threatens or intimidates people. The term is usually applied to children and adolescents, and consists of behavior that violates social norms and is disruptive, often distressing others more than it does the person demonstrating the behaviors (Miller-Keane Encyclopedia and Dictionary of Medicine, Nursing, and Allied Health, Seventh Edition, 2003). Very specifically, the Diagnostic and Statistical Manual- Fifth Edition defines disruptive behaviors as part of the Disruptive Behavior Disorder

NOS (not otherwise specified). Symptoms of Disruptive Behavior Disorder include the following: Consistent defiance of authoritative figures, the Inability to take responsibility for bad behavior. Temper tantrums on a regular basis and vengeful behavior and resentment are included. Aggressiveness toward people or animals destroying the property of others. Stealing and lying bullying, and finally constant rule breaking are all included. In some instances, verbal aggressions are very harmful to children and adolescents, in particular. Negative self-talk and negative verbalizations with others that reflect internalized racial oppression can be destructive to the healthy ego development, self-esteem and self -concept of people. Young people without the internal resources to counter insults and false statements, can internalize these aggressions and demonstrate maladaptive behaviors. The game the "Dozens", which is a game of "mother" insults is an example of deleterious behavior that is familiar to many urban students.

SCHOOL CLIMATE

School climate refers to the quality and character of school life. School climate is based on patterns of students', parents' and school personnel's experience of school life and reflects norms, goals, values, interpersonal relationships, teaching and learning practices, and organizational structures. A sustainable, positive school climate fosters youth development and learning necessary for a productive, contributing and satisfying life in a democratic society. This climate includes norms, values and expectations that support people feeling socially, emotionally and physically safe. People are engaged and respected. Students, families, and educators work together to develop, live and contribute to a shared school vision. Educators model and nurture attitudes that emphasize the benefits and satisfaction gained from learning. Each person contributes to the operations of the school and the care of the physical environment (National School Climate Council *2015*). Synthesizing past school climate research as well as NSCC's research efforts, the National School Climate Council and NSCC suggest that there are four major areas that school climate assessment needs to include: Safety; with subheadings Rules and Norms, Sense of Physical Security and Sense of Social/Emotional Security. The next major area is entitled Interpersonal-Relationships, Respect for Diversity and Social Supports for both Adults and Students. The third major category is Teaching and Learning with support for learning, as a sub- category along with social and civic learning. The fourth category is the external environment, which include institutional environment, and staff only items. Leadership and professional relationships are also sub - categories in the fourth area. The final category is entitled institutional environment, with the subheadings school connectedness or engagement and physical surroundings. Considering the neighborhood school with a magnet school designation, in which the Intervention will be conducted, there are areas of concern in the assessment of school climate.

The Intervention District Public School, located in a northern, New Jersey community, enjoys the benefits of a wonderfully diverse population. Artists, business leaders, community activists and many others find comfort and adventure in this community.

Not unlike many others in the country, it is stratified with affluent people in one area and those in poverty in another. Since this is the case, the public school system attempts to offer a vast array of opportunities to provide service. Families in the region have become so confident and comfortable with educational offerings in the Intervention district, that they have settled here, even from communities nearby like Newark and as far away as White Plains, New York. A small district, the Intervention District Public Schools are closely aligned with a prominent State University which has a very busy Learning Assessment clinic. This association provides unique opportunity to learn about specific people in and from many surrounding areas.

The Intervention school is similar to many schools which serve urban students in that there is a stratified protocol. That is, the experiences of student of African descent is significantly more punitive and injurious than the educational experiences of others (Skiba 2002). In too many instances virtually identical and sometimes even more disruptive actions from students are managed in a completely skewed way. One of the factors that makes this possible is the level of parental presence in the school building and parent and teacher interaction (National School Climate Council 2015).

Sense of Physical Security

Generally, staff and students feel safe from potentially harmful outside entities. However, The Achiever Program with whom the intervention will be conducted is an in-district, "out-of-district" therapeutic support program. Students, who are all males of color are routinely physically removed from classrooms and carried or coerced into the "time out room". This spectacle occurs so often that many students seem desensitized to it for the program members, but when asked if they thought it appropriate for all students, respond in the negative.

Sense of Social-Emotional Security

The line of demarcation for the Intervention school experience free from verbal injury and emotional compromise is split along lines of affluence and disadvantage. Faculty and staff have been engaged in training for Response to Intervention focused instruction and behavior management. That reality has placed an enormous burden on some educators who find themselves unable to meet an effective teaching standard. Consequently, the interpersonal climate was tense and heavy with anxiety.

Support for Learning

What is realized about the learning climate is that in many cases the individual attention students might receive is directly proportional to the time adult family members spent in service to the school. Children of families with adult members who can volunteer to assist teachers during traditional school hours receive more positive individual attention than other children whose adult family members are unable to provide the same type of support.

Respect for Diversity

As important as the district and building leadership said that diversity is as a goal in schools and in the community, almost all certificated staff is not of color in the district. Several professionals of color have been hired to work in the building. The larger community is looking forward to reflections of those new professionals in the educational practices in the building as per district goals.

School Connectedness/Engagement

It may be the case that some students and staff felt connected to the school and engaged by teaching and learning practices in the building, however those among the most- needy did not. In fact, many of the most -needy families felt alienated from school and would not communicate with professionals. When some professionals began to visit families in their homes this was improved.

CREATIVE ARTS

Creative arts therapies include art therapy, music therapy, dance movement therapy, drama therapy and psychodrama along with focus on the creative and expressive process of creating art. Before now, creative arts therapies or CAT's were considered great for well- being and growth. This research includes focus on the vital use of CAT's for diagnostic and therapeutic purposes (Zwerling 1979). As we learn more about the empirically present efficacy of CAT's we recognize that we have used music, for example to change or even improve mood. What we are seeing now is that CAT's can be used in a more methodical way to achieve predictable results regularly. Among the several modalities considered emerging and promising for treatment of torture survivors are modalities that insist that impact be understood by the context of the person experiencing the suffering. Art therapy, dance/movement therapy, drama, music and ritual are among the somatic therapies considered at the core of the healing mechanism for torture survivors. According to Terr and Herman (2008), traumatic memory is based in imagery and body sensation moreover, lacking verbal narrative. The ability to use music therapy interventions to express those feelings, thoughts and emotions that are not easily expressed in words is in fact a kind of emotional maturation.

Dance/Movement Therapy

Dance/Movement Therapy or DMT is considered basic to human expression and in fact a "primary language for all human beings, which is both somatic and expressive". Ritual in continental African and African- Caribbean communities are found to result in the outcome of "discharging aggression and restoring interpersonal connection". Aspects of poverty and its implications are similar to torture in that both experiences traumatize the child. Treatment of torture, including poverty, necessitates a more holistic approach. That is, according to Gray, the physical, mental, social, emotional, spiritual, contextual, cultural, and familial, etc. parts of the whole person. Oppression, by definition restricts the physical, social/emotional and psychic movement of the oppressed person. Liberation from that oppressed state requires the removal of the perceived boundary for total human expression.

Therapy

Music therapy is the clinical and evidence-based use of music to accomplish therapeutic goals. Several trials and reviews have determined that music therapy is beneficial for several goals. They include, but are not limited to motor skills, social/interpersonal skills and cognitive development, self- awareness, pain control, reducing anxiety, stress, anger and agitation, and improving mood states (Choi, Lee & Jung-Sook, 2007). A review of the music therapy literature delineates at least three broad domains of functioning where music therapy has been successfully used in the treatment of emotionally disturbed children: affect regulation, communication and social/behavior dysfunction (Hussey, 2004). Specific interventions that seem to be most helpful in therapy include playing musical instruments, both, melodic and percussive; listening to music, singing songs, song writing and song drawing, which encourages children to create pictures while listening to music.

In music therapy, specifically, treatments may include creating, singing, listening to and/or moving to music in order to strengthen client's abilities. According to Lev-Wiesel et. al. (2012), the Creative arts can be enjoyable, but they are not principally recreational or instructional lessons. Clients don't need previous experience or proficiency in an area for it to be useful in treatment. Creativity and imagination along with a degree of playfulness and holism contribute to the very real abilities to cope, solve problems, integrate the mind and body, grow and develop more vitality. Clients are better able to express emotions and feelings, inner difficulties, bypass dissociative mechanisms and even encourage verbalization.

RHYTHMIC ENTRAINMENT

The concept of greater individual and group awareness is central to the mechanism of action for this Intervention. Entrainment encapsulates the goals of awareness and regulation, an appropriate response to stimuli, balanced by the learner himself. Rhythmic Entrainment Intervention is an auditory program that uses musical rhythm to stimulate and re-pattern neurological function. The developer, Jeff Strong is an ethnomusicologist who has identified hundreds of rhythmic combinations that correspond to specific behavioral and cognitive symptoms. Listening to specific rhythmic patterns elicits immediate calming and focusing effects, and repeated exposure to these rhythms often results in long-term behavioral and cognitive improvements. These improvements are generally seen in three to four weeks. This intervention technique uses a diagnostic survey, custom made CD's, promises to revise those

CD's if the desired results are not seen, and provides on line and manual training for practitioners. The program can be administered in the home or school, does not require headphones, is compatible with other therapies and will not negatively affect anyone who hears it.

Among the improvement areas for this program are less hyperactivity and impulsivity, increased learning ability, a longer attention span, better social skills, less aggression and anxiety and better sleep. The discovery of the concept of entrainment is credited to Dutch scientist Christian Huygens who used pendulum clocks in 1665 (Friedman, 2000). He found that if two pendulum clocks were placed side by side, by the next day their pendulums would swing in unison. Similarly, when drummers play they become entrained. Through rhythmic repetition of ritual sounds, the bodies, brains and nervous systems of the players are energized and transformed.

African Cultural Arts (ACA)

It is appropriate that notwithstanding the Maafa and other traumatic experiences of people of African descent, the gifts of the ancient culture still have relevance in achieving whole-ness for Africans and others throughout the diaspora. The cooperation of Africans in the diaspora has helped contemporary Africans and others around the world know what the ancient Africans did in their societies. Even though the African drum was once an illegal instrument for people of color in this country, now members of all ethnic groups can benefit from its use. An African Cultural Arts Program (ACA) can be effective in that it may incorporate music and creative arts interventions. In addition to playing and singing songs from the Old Malian Empire, which are lyrically sound and meaningful for teaching coping skills, children will become familiar with the geography, languages, foods, rituals, clothing, natural resources, institutions of governing, values, norms and other aspects of the culture.

Childhood aggression has become a major concern to psychosocial development in youth. Treatment for aggressive behavior includes techniques that reduce impulsive behavior. Studies with adults show that music therapy provides opportunities for enhancing a sense of control over emotions through catharsis. Children with highly aggressive behavior, find that aggression is reduced and self-esteem is improved with group music intervention. Longitudinal studies have demonstrated that early childhood aggression has a relatively high likelihood of persistence over time. Narrowly focused treatment approaches provide less enduring positive changes than comprehensive interventions. The understanding of developmental psychopathology has been strengthened with the emergence of risk and resiliency as a framework to predict psychosocial outcomes in aggressive youth. The question becomes what has more influence, risk or the protective factors.

Empirical evidence shows the value of protective factors that encourage resilience in children and adolescents. Psychiatric symptoms would be less predictive than risk and protective factors for outcomes, and risk would be less predictive of outcomes than protective factors. The research design included experimental methods in a longitudinal study. Participants were evaluated annually for four years. Children under age 18 who became state certified as chronically or severely aggressive, who had a neurological or psychiatric disorder, and who had been placed in public custody or excluded from access to needed treatment and educational services were included. One hundred nine participants were classified as low performers. One hundred twelve were classified as high performers. Initial psychiatric symptom severity was not predictive of outcomes. However, early childhood aggression during earlier school years was a significant predictor of poor behavioral outcomes. Risk and resilience mechanisms continue to moderate outcomes, even at very high levels of risk and in the presence of severe disorder.

DANCE

What is the feasibility, acceptability and potential efficacy of after school dance classes, and family based intervention to reduce television viewing, thereby reducing weight gain among African American girls? Modes of dance that affirm African American girls will potentially improve the health and self-concept of girls in central city educational settings. In addition, the dance classes paired with reduced television viewing may have a positive impact on the self- esteem of African American school- aged girls. Prior research suggested that introducing African American girls to culturally specific dancing, while reducing television viewing would be a feasible, acceptable and potentially effective way to reduce weight gain in African American girls. Since many barriers exist to the weight reduction intervention that are specific to African American girls and women it was necessary to find an intervention that provided opportunities for immediate positive feedback, moderate to vigorous physical activity, and a connection to the social, cultural and historical importance of dance in the African community. Dance is one of the only art forms that survived transplantation to the United States, slavery and social oppression.

AFRICAN WELLNESS

The African American Wellness Village uses a model of cultural sensitivity to provide access to free health screenings and generally couple the African American community members with health care opportunities. More than half of the participants say that this health care event is the only place that they received screenings, and the sensitive environment inspired trust. For this reason, those respondents preferred the screenings at the Wellness Village. As a result of the work of the African American Health Coalition, Inc. (AAHC) attention has been called to the great health disparities among people in Oregon. The Disparities have been documented in the *Report of the Secretary's Task Force on Black and minority Health* (1985). The Wellness Village was founded by a group of volunteers that included both black health professionals and advocates who organized to fight the social injustice that is a factor in health disparities in Oregon. According to the authors, the Portland African American community is easily mobilized when approached by individuals whom they trust. This may also be true of other predominantly African communities in the country. The AAHC has demonstrated commitment to the community it was designed to serve. The annual Wellness Village has become a relied upon opportunity for health education, preventive screenings, and links to resources and referral information. It is a major community event.

In order to encourage families of low-income youth to overcome stigma and other negative attitudes about treatment interventions need to target low income youth and actually have a positive development approach of increasing core characteristics that can influence a wide range of problem behaviors. Group drumming is one of those interventions. It is inclusive, non-verbal, is universal, and does not require prior experience for participation. It still has room, though to develop proficiency and mastery within the discipline. Group drumming is culturally relevant, and supports the value of collectivism present in many Eastern- based cultures. Reflection and self- disclosure have been considered activities that help to reduce stress. Group drumming encourages these stress relievers and has been shown to have a bio- psychosocial efficacy to that end.

Neuroendocrine and immune changes showed reduced stress levels in adults, improved mood, and reduced burnout in long term care nurses and improved social-emotional functioning in adolescents living in a court-referred residential treatment center. According to Social Cognitive Theory, group drumming combined with group counseling activities would encourage self-efficacy and positive outcome expectations through enactive attainment, vicarious experience, verbal persuasion and reduction of physiological arousal. Chronic stress is an area that requires innovative interventions in low-income youth and their families. School based group drumming is a low cost, easily accessible, culturally relevant activity that coupled with activities from group counseling, could improve social and emotional behavior in low income children. Traditional African conceptualizations of illness and health integrate social, spiritual, physical and mental realms, all of which are impacted by trauma when it occurs. According to the author, the African worldview places dance as a conduit of individual and community healing. The underlying belief is that in the community, mind and body must be incorporated into ritual systems in order to facilitate healing, as well as to transform and empower the individual and the group. Rituals play an integral role in socialization, expression and communication. They help to build and maintain a healthy sense of self system, and offer an alternative cathartic experience for individuals and the community.

The philosophical perspective of the historic African tradition centers on holism and socio-cultural and psycho-spiritual themes. Movement, especially when it is placed within ritual, may be a natural way to address problems that develop. The suppression of dance in many cultures has resulted in an imbalance in those spiritual, communal and interpersonal qualities that regulate the individual and unify societies. According to Hanna (1987), dance represents a physical instrument or symbol for feeling/ and or thoughts that can serve as a more effective medium than verbal language in revealing ones needs and desires. In essence, using the dance as a healing tool is in fact restoring part of the historic balancing system (Maat) that Africans have used for thousands of years.

Children who have difficulty integrating themselves within traditional scholastic programs are sometimes called "at risk". These children are particularly vulnerable to gang influences and often display angry, aggressive, sometimes anxious and often hostile behavior at school and in the community. If these children could become less aggressive and anxious, they might be able to participate more effectively in their learning at school. If these vulnerable children found success in their traditional school environments, especially in the academic disciplines that can assist in successful post high school experiences, they might find themselves in a better position to transform their lives and communities in healthy ways. According to Choi et al. (2007), the benefits of music therapy which include improved motor skills, social/interpersonal skills, cognitive development, self- awareness, pain control, reducing anxiety, stress, anger, agitation, and improved mood states are well established. A review of the music therapy literature delineates at least three broad domains of functioning within which music therapy has been successfully used in the treatment of emotionally disturbed children: 1) affect regulation, 2) communication and 3) social/ behavior dysfunction. (Hussey, 2004). Many children of African heritage may be able to trace their ancestry to the Old Malian Empires of Western Africa, which include

Senegal, Nigeria, Mali, Benin, Liberia, Sierra Leone, Ghana, Burkina Faso, Guinea, the Ivory Coast, Niger, Cameroon and Togo. The population of students from many communities' lack connection to their heritage as a result of Maafa.

Learning about African cultures before the Triangular Slave Trade, and specifically, a focus on the celebrations of life, can reawaken curiosity about learning, and help to develop self-regulation skills. These celebrations include the focus upon physically and emotionally handicapped people within the community and celebrate birth, death, various rites of passage, child naming, harvest reaping and great suffering among other major life events. These efforts teach resilience in very under-standable and simple ways. Such interventions are feasible and sometimes organizations in the community, both civic and business, sponsor cultural area programs, as they do sports and recreational programs.

Educators become able to design music programs that meet specific needs and address concerns directly when we define the roles and importance of music education in the lives of at-risk children. Very little work has been done with at-risk students, especially with music education. Research (Choi, Lee & Jung-Sook, 2007) has shown that it has a positive effect on re-acclimating students to the educative process. Students in an American mid-west community who were enrolled in a large, urban alternative school for the arts, their teachers and parents were involved in the study.

There were 139 in the academic category, 120 in the adjust-ment and behavior category, 102 in the school setting for at-risk classification, 68 for the home and family risk, and 40 in the physical and mental health risk groups. Student self-perceptions were measured both by means of pre-intervention test and a post- test after a period of 16 weeks with the "Self-Perception Profile for Children." The summaries of each student's participation resulted in three general categories of outcomes. Students either showed some improvement over time of the intervention with observable decreases in at risk characteristics, showed no observable changes in either direction, or grew observably worse. Music education was found to be helpful but the promise of performance was sometimes a chaotic confounding variable. The therapeutic value of music creation and participation does not rest in one's ability to perform, but in one's ability to function. Performance pressures can cause distress and are not necessary to enjoy therapeutic value.

The mental health care and child welfare fields have been looking for effective therapies to use with victimized children, especially those suffering with post- traumatic stress disorder and treated with cognitive behavioral therapy. A concerning gap in the literature is that many emotionally-disturbed children suffer from cognitive deficits and developmental disabilities. Music is ideally suited to fill this gap. Since direct therapeutic work can be difficult for children in this population, music has the potential to bypass the defensive operations of the higher cortical functions of the brain and move directly to the limbic system where emotions are processed. When clinicians can take what is evident in experimental settings and make those experiences viable in natural settings, we have advanced the field by generalizing the therapeutic technique. Several case studies were examined that assessed the effectiveness of music therapy with children and adolescents of all ages. Typical techniques included in music therapy include free and structured improvisation, singing familiar songs or improvised ones, listening to music and verbal reflection of the musical processes as it related to the client's problems. According to several researchers, improvisation was seen as central in most cases. The use of pre-composed music and other songs were described as activities that could be used to create a safe and familiar environment. In order to encourage families of low-income youth to overcome stigma and other negative attitudes about treatment for well-established psychological risk factors and for behavior problems and school failure, interventions need to target low income youth and actually have a positive development approach of increasing core characteristics that can influence a wide range of problem behaviors.

Resilience

Resilience is at its foundation, the relationship between internal state and external experiences. Resilience derives from supportive relationships, adaptive capacities, and positive experiences. We can see and measure resilience in terms of how students' brains, immune systems, and genes all respond to stressful experiences. There is a common set of characteristics that predispose children to positive outcomes in the face of adversity.

Important elements for enhanced resilience include, the availability of at least one stable, caring, and supportive relationship between a child and an adult caregiver. A sense of mastery over life circumstances is critical. Strong executive function and self-regulation skills are helpful. The supportive context of affirming faith or cultural traditions helps to stabilize one's life. Finally, learning to cope with manageable threats to our physical and social well-being is also critical for the development of resilience. Some children demonstrate greater sensitivity to both negative and positive experiences. Resilience can be situation-specific. Positive and negative experiences over time continue to influence a child's mental and physical development. Resilience can be built; it's not only an innate trait or a resource that can be used up. People's responses to stressful experiences varies dramatically, but extreme adversity nearly always generates serious problems that require treatment.

The implications for research that explores the fostering and analysis of resilience in children are far reaching. Educators know in real terms that children are resilient, but if we can isolate the process by which they demonstrate resilience, we can teach it to people who may not access their abilities so easily. In addition, we can enhance the resilience process by providing for and developing the proactive factors that encourage resilient living.

Early clinical case descriptions provide some direction in understanding why some children are able to cope with adversity whereas others are unable. Invulnerable and stress resistant are two terms used to describe cases described by Bleuler and Anthony (1984 and 1987).

People who cope well in pro-social situations are described by Murphy and Moriarty (1976) compliment the longitudinal studies conducted by Rutter, (1987) which is now a four-decade long study of high risk infants born into poverty on the Hawaiian island of Kauai. These provided good groundwork for emerging research. Evidence suggests that children can recover and develop normally and Masten (2001) challenged the idea that resilient children have developed special qualities. She suggests instead that resilience is in effect normal and can be taught. Authors concluded that resilience should be seen as an acquired, gradually internalized, generalized set of attributes that enable a person to adapt to life's difficult circumstances. Resilience is a skill and can be taught and enhanced with support of proactive factors.

Summary

Acquired skills can assist students in navigating away from harmful involvement and toward helpful community involvement that indicates healthy self-esteem and self-concept. In order to encourage families of low-income youth to overcome stigma and other negative attitudes about treatment for well-established psychological risk factors for behavior problems and school failure, interventions need to target low income youth and actually have a positive development approach of increasing core characteristics that can influence a wide range of problem behaviors.

Group drumming is one of those interventions. It is inclusive, non-verbal, universal, does not require prior experience for participation, and still has room to develop proficiency and mastery within the discipline. Group drumming is culturally relevant, and supports the value of collectivism present in many Eastern- based cultures.

Reflection and self-disclosure have been considered activities that help to reduce stress. Group drumming encourages these stress relievers and has been shown to have a bio-psychosocial efficacy to that end. Chronic stress is an area that requires innovative interventions to address in low-income youth and their families. School based group drumming is a low cost, easily accessible, culturally relevant activity that coupled with activities from group counseling could improve social and emotional behavior in low income children.

CHAPTER 3

METHODOLOGY

INTRODUCTION

Poverty significantly impacts children in urban schools. As a result, children in central city schools as well as their families demonstrate the symptoms of learned helplessness. Among those symptoms is low self- esteem. In many instances, children do not see the value of school or the educative process. Many children do not see school as a viable method for achieving the things they want from life. Since some students are not able to benefit from the school experience in tangible and meaningful ways, they are disappointed and can become a disruptive presence.

THE INTERVENTION

A review of the music therapy literature delineates at least three broad domains of functioning where music therapy has been successfully used in the treatment of emotionally disturbed children. Affect regulation, communication, and social/behavior dysfunction (Hussey, 2004) are those areas. Specific interventions that seem to be most helpful in therapy include playing musical instruments, listening to music, singing songs, song writing and song drawing, which encourages children to create pictures while listening to music.

Several activities comprised the ACA Intervention, conducted over a 60- day period. There were eight, 40-minute drumming sessions. A 40- minute individual counseling session took place for each learner once a week. A 40-minute group counseling session, during which goals were discussed took place on the Friday of each week. In addition, the Individual Education Plan goals included for students were plans that include greater self- awareness, good self- expression and self-regulation (CBC). We saw the reduction and elimination of aggressive and disruptive outbursts. Data detailing the aggressive and disruptive behavior before and after the Intervention suggest that it made a positive difference in the elimination of those outbursts.

The ACA drumming sessions were conducted as a part of the general education curricula music program. The newly constructed elementary intervention school served students Kindergarten through grade 5. The work period of active drumming was 30 to 40 minutes. Orienting, descriptions of instruments, rhythms and their origins took place for 5 minutes each week. Contemporary adaptations, songs and accompanying dress descriptions took place for 5 minutes. Thursday afternoons, immediately after lunch, each learner participated in a group drumming session, taught by an African drum instructor. The soft, understated disposition of the male instructor served as a marvelous model of self- regulation and control of temperament that was encouraged as a goal of the M.A.P curriculum. Instruments and rhythms associated with, the Old Malian Empire, the country of Brazil, island of Cuba, territory of Puerto Rico, and finally hip hop were particularly interesting to the students.

Descriptive Analysis

A total number of 40 surveys were distributed, with 32 surveys appropriately completed. Eight surveys were excluded because they were incomplete, were completed by only parents or were not received by the appropriate date. The children were grouped according to their special education classification: Emotionally disturbed. According to the New Jersey statute Title: 18: A; emotionally disturbed is defined in the following ways. These students' educational performance is adversely affected by one or more of the following; an inability to learn that cannot be explained by intellectual, sensory, or health factors. Next, an inability to build or maintain satisfactory interpersonal relationships with peers and teachers. Next, inappropriate behaviors or feelings under normal circumstances. Emotionally disturbed children demonstrate a general pervasive mood of unhappiness or depression. Finally, they display a tendency to develop physical symptoms or fears associated with personal or school problems.

In almost every instance, the emotionally disturbed criteria was violated and made this particular classification inappropriate for each of the participants. Most of the learner problems stemmed from poverty. Since legal and educational policies seem to make this classifying process helpful, it was used. The learners classify themselves as African American or Black. The active participants were ten years old. The ten-year-old participants were formally enrolled in grade five, and functioned on varying reading levels. The range of reading level included second grade mastery to seventh grade mastery. The study allowed four learners to disclose the taking of mood stabilizing or psychotropic medicine as per medical treatment. Seven students lived with caretakers who were not the learner's biological parents. One student saw his mother murdered by his father. One student was living with a foster parent. Eight students received social services beyond those provided in school, and all of the students had some experience with physical restraint in school. See table 1.

Frequency of Gender of Participants

Gender	Frequency	%
Female	0	0
Male	32	100
Total	32	100

Table 1

MEASURES AND PROCEDURES

Child Behavior Checklist for ages 6-18 Aggressive Behaviors and Disruptive Impulses data were used. Due to varying levels of reading comprehension, words were explained and defined. In every case the learner knew the purpose of this study and provided informed assent and full cooperation. Parental consent was also included. The students were curious about the prospect of improving their school and home functioning. They seemed to want to become acquainted with artistic expression in general and specifically group drumming.

This was a quantitative study using the paired samples approach. In, n = 32, the student's levels of disruptive behaviors were assessed in pre and post tests using the twenty question portion of The Child Behavior Checklist for ages 6-18 Aggressive Behaviors and Disruptive Impulses (CBCL), which was completed by parents and teachers, to measure individual levels of self-concept.

ANALYSIS

The findings from the Child Behavior Checklist for ages 6-18 Aggressive Behaviors and Disruptive Impulses, surveys were statistically examined on SPSS 22. The study utilized repeated measures analysis, specifically the dependent t- test. To provide answers to specific research questions, descriptive and inferential statistics were calculated.

Analyses were based on data from 32 fifth grade, classified emotionally impaired, males. The M. A. program, a special education experimental course of study (an in district, out of district more flexible and therapeutic program), included curricula consistent with the New Jersey Core Curriculum Content Standards for fifth grade learners. Group therapy, individual counseling, restraining, intense parental communication, speech therapy, occupational therapy, communication with private therapists, and social work intervention were included.

STATISTICAL ANALYSIS

This study was conducted using archival data consisting of parent and teacher, ratings. Statistical analyses were conducted using a dependent t - test with repeated measures. The .01 level ($\alpha = .01$) was used to determine statistical significance. The data were derived from pre and post administrations of the twenty question portion of the Child Behavior Checklist for ages 6-18 Aggressive Behaviors and Disruptive Impulses.

Dr. Tammarra R. Jones

Summary

Many children do not see school as a viable method for achieving the things they want from life. Since some students are not able to benefit from the school experience in tangible and meaningful ways, they are disappointed and can become a disruptive presence. A review of the music therapy literature delineates at least three broad domains of functioning where music therapy has been successfully used in the treatment of emotionally disturbed children. Affect regulation, communication and social/behavior dysfunction are those areas (Hussey, 2004). The Child Behavior Checklist Aggression Problem Scale (CBCL) was used to measure learner aggressive disruptions to the learning session. After the testing period, self-esteem improved and aggressiveness was reduced. This was a quantitative study using the, paired samples, repeated measures approach.

Drums have been used very successfully with at-risk adolescents in high schools (Friedman, 2000). Drums are a very natural way of helping adolescents deal with anger for a number of reasons: drumming is a peer-respected activity, drumming is fun. Drumming provides a means of releasing suppressed emotions, and drumming helps to develop a stronger concept of self-worth (Friedman, 2000).

CHAPTER 4

RESULTS

INTRODUCTION

This study was conducted to determine if the ACA intervention results showed significant reductions in aggressive and disruptive behaviors over time. In every instance, students demonstrated that the weekly drumming and orienting sessions made positive differences in their aggressive and disruptive behavior.

RESEARCH QUESTION AND HYPOTHESIS

This study addressed the following research questions: Can 30 minutes of participation in African Cultural Arts, specifically drumming weekly, decrease disruptive and impulsive behaviors in African American male students? Can the ACA intervention help move students from a more restrictive learning environment to a less restrictive learning environment? Can students become re-engaged in the learning process and more interested in school as a means for enhancing their lives, as a result of participating in the ACA program?

Hypothesis - Through drumming and the ACA program, it is expected that students will reduce aggressive and disruptive impulses and behaviors. Students will become re-engaged or encouraged to see the schooling process as more beneficial than not. Students may even become more likely to become transformed "life-long" learners.

SOURCE OF ARCHIVED DATA

In order to provide rewards for less aggression and disruption, those data were collected and analyzed. The district director of special services granted permission for the author to analyze the data. School leadership also granted permission to analyze data. Those data are saved and were a part of the school record for each child.

STUDENT PROGRAM THAT PROVIDED THE DATA FOR ANALYSIS

The M. A. program is a special education experimental course of study (an in district, out of district, more flexible, therapeutic program), which included curricula consistent with the New Jersey Core Curriculum Content Standards for fifth grade learners. In addition, group therapy, individual counseling, physical restraining, intense parental communication, speech therapy, occupational therapy, communications with private therapists, and social work interventions were included. See Table 2.

Type of Therapeutic Activity	Frequency	Percent
Speech Therapy	17	53.1%
Occupational Therapy	32	100%
Individual Counseling	15	46.8%
Group Counseling	32	100%
Intense Parental Communication	32	100%
Communication with Private Therapist	12	38%
Interventions Beyond School	20	62.5%

Note: N= 32

Table 2

Portions of Child Behavior Checklist for ages 6-18 Aggressive Behaviors and Disruptive Impulses, which reflected aggression and disruptive impulses were chosen. Twenty questions were answered by parents and teachers. Questions that focused on physical, social/emotional, internalizing and externalizing behaviors were analyzed in this study.

Among the physical behavior items were questions that included physical attacks on others, clinging to adults, cruelty to animals, bullying, fighting, screaming and threatening people. Social/Emotional behavior questions focused on behaviors like a willingness to talk, lying, maturation level, clowning, and using profanity. Internalizing behaviors focused on behaviors that signaled fear of failure, and obsessive anxiety, finger sucking, having a hot temper, being suspicious and demanding attention. Finally, external behaviors like being with troubled children, vandalism and whining were analyzed. In each of the four areas; physical, social/emotional, internalizing and externalizing behaviors were significantly reduced according to parent and teacher ratings on the post Child Behavior Checklist for Ages 6-18 test. Statistics Results are presented in Table 3.

Child Behavior Checklist Pre and Post Test Differences

Behaviors	Mean Difference	Standard Deviation	t-Value	Significance Level	Cohen's d
Act too Young for Age	-1.59	.49	18.07	p<.000	3.19
Clingy	-.53	.50	5.92	p<.000	.97
Cruel to Animals	-.34	.60	3.23	p<.003	.57
Bullying	-.34	.60	3.23	p<.003	.57
Demands Attention	-1.12	.90	7.01	p<.000	1.24
Perfection	-.87	.70	7.00	p<.000	1.23
Fights	-.87	.87	5.68	p<.000	1.00
Hangs with Trouble	-.90	.68	7.44	p<.000	1.31
Lying	-1.40	.66	11.95	p<.000	2.19
Physically Attacks	-1.21	.70	9.76	p<.000	1.72
Refuses to Talk	-.56	.75	4.19	p<.000	.74
Screams	-1.0	.95	5.95	p<.000	1.05
Clowning	-1.40	.75	10.52	p<.000	1.86
Suspicious	-1.18	.99	6.73	p<.000	1.18
Profanity	-.71	.85	4.77	p<.000	.84
Hot Tempered	-.53	.84	3.57	p<.001	.63
Threatens People	-.53	.76	3.94	p<.000	.69
Finger Sucking	-1.06	.94	6.33	p<.000	1.12
Vandalism	-1.06	.71	8.39	p<.000	1.48
Whining	-1.5	.76	11.13	p<.000	1.96

Table 3

In order to determine if aggressive behaviors and disruptive impulses were reduced as per Child Behavior Checklist for Ages 6-18 based Aggressive Behaviors and Disruptive Impulses, scores were completed by parents and teachers of the 32 fifth grade, 10- year - old boys, a dependent t-test was conducted in each of the twenty areas determined to reflect physical, social/emotional, internalizing and externalizing behaviors.

PHYSICAL BEHAVIOR RESULTS

Results revealed that aggressive physical behaviors were reduced as per the Child Behavior Checklist for ages 6-18 Aggressive Behaviors and Disruptive Impulses scores. The fifth grade boys were less clingy to adults, were less cruel to animals, engaged in less bullying and fewer fights at home and in school. Physical attacks on other people occurred much less frequently, and screaming as a means of expression stopped. The participants threatened people much less often. One child who had developed larger breasts as a result of psychotropic medicine side effects began to wear more formal clothes to school each day (a shirt and tie) ostensibly to affirm his maleness and to "appear more serious about life."

SOCIAL/EMOTIONAL DEFICIT RESULTS

Results also revealed that social/emotional deficits were reduced. The children in the study did not appear as immature to parents and teachers. They lied much less often, very rarely refused to talk, were not heard being profane most of the time, and eliminated "Clowning" behaviors all together.

INTERNALIZING BEHAVIOR RESULTS

Internalizing behaviors including the demand of attention from teachers and parents at home and at school were also reduced as per post- test Child Behavior Checklist for Ages 6-18 scores. Suspiciousness was reduced. Boys who had demonstrated "Hot Tempers" were rated as eliminating those behaviors. In 100% of the sample, physical expressions of anger were reduced. Long term analysis of these participants would be helpful in determining if these reductions were indeed changed or adjusted for parents and teachers. Children who had been observed to suck their fingers, perhaps indicating an inappropriate level of immaturity were not observed doing this when post test results were collected.

Externalizing Behavior Results

Finally, external behaviors including spending time with troubled children, vandalism and whining were reduced with whining almost eliminated from observed behavior. Concentrated efforts to correct these behaviors including the engaging of the hands and senses with group drumming, seems to have made a positive difference in the lives of the fifth grade, African American boys in the short term (after 60 days).

Summary of Results

Results of this study show that aggressive and disruptive impulses as evidenced by behavior, can be effectively reduced with 30 minutes of drumming, weekly, within an African Cultural Arts Therapeutic program for learners classified as emotionally disturbed. The three variables of drumming, group and individual counseling worked to enhance these children's former behavioral problems.

CHAPTER 5

——————

DISCUSSION

INTRODUCTION

The purpose of the study was to determine if 30 minutes of group drumming could reduce aggressive behaviors and disruptive impulses in African American males classified as emotionally disturbed in the fifth grade of an experimental, therapeutic, public school program. It was hypothesized that the drumming would reduce aggressive behaviors and disruptive impulses. The results of the study suggest that aggressive behaviors and disruptive impulses were significantly reduced.

DISCUSSION OF RESULTS

The philosophical basis for developing the activities that were a part of the African Cultural Arts program came from the principle of Maat. Maat is an ancient Egyptian principle that included truth, balance, order harmony, law, morality and justice. The doctrine of Maat is carved in stone in Egypt and contained in the Papyrus of Ani, translated by Budge in 1895.

The concept of Maat is often referred to as the 42 negative confessions, and is the template for functioning in this world and the next, according to Memphite theology. Among the 42 statements that are the negative confessions are declarations about not lying, not using profanity, being balanced in disposition (not having a hot temper), not physically attacking people, and not acting with evil rage. These guides for living were taught to the study participants and discussed during a part of the group therapy sessions held Friday of each week. Most of the participants were familiar with the Ten Commandments and the golden rule, so that when they learned that Maat predated those guides and came from African people in ancient Egypt they were open to examining them weekly.

In addition to natural maturity, rewards in school and at home for constructive behavior, and role models both in history and in their own community, the understanding and examination of the principle of Maat helped the participants to change their behavior as observed by parents and teachers.

The participants were expected to be positively impacted by the group drumming intervention. That is, aggressive behaviors and disruptive impulses were expected to be reduced as a result of the weekly group drumming class in the context of the experimental, therapeutic in-district program. The results suggest that disruptive impulses and aggressive behaviors subsided as evidenced by the significant decrease in behaviors including screaming, the demonstration of a hot temper, lying, being cruel to animals, physically attacking people, bullying, fighting and threatening people as observed by teachers and parents. With regard to the four areas of behavior; physical, social/emotional, internalizing and externalizing all showed significant reductions as identified by parents and teachers via The Child Behavior Checklist for ages 6-18 Aggressive Behaviors and Disruptive Impulses. A large part of the individual counseling process taught the importance of self-reflection. Participants were encouraged to take time to examine their feelings and consider how their behaviors might be perceived by parents, teachers and others in the school community. Once participants became more aware of how they were presenting themselves, they became more skilled at regulating their aggressive behaviors and disruptive impulses. This activity in particular was very effective in modifying aggressive behaviors and disruptive impulses. Participants were taught to examine themselves and record their authentic feelings in journals and audio recordings like spoken word or music selections regularly. This was very helpful in tracking progress or regression and provided good evidence for actual change. Group drumming was helpful in participant progress. As participant's behavior improved their drumming compatibility also changed. Participants developed preferences for drumming partners and had insight about why they preferred to drum with some other participants. As preferences became clearer, sound improved and was reinforcing for more effort toward participant's self-regulation of aggressive behaviors and disruptive impulses.

PHYSICAL BEHAVIORS

Seven of the Child Behavior Checklist for ages 6-18 Aggressive Behaviors and Disruptive Impulses questions addressed physical behaviors including threatening people, being cruel to animals, clinging to adults, bullying others, fighting, physically attacking people, and screaming to communicate. All of the behaviors were reduced and screaming to communicate was eliminated.

SOCIAL/EMOTIONAL BEHAVIORS

Five of the questions addressed social/emotional behaviors. Clowning, acting too young for one's age, lying, refusing to talk, and profanity were all reduced. Clowning as observed by parents and teachers was eliminated.

INTERNALIZING BEHAVIORS

Five of the questions from the Child Behavior Checklist for ages 6-18 Aggressive Behaviors and Disruptive Impulses addressed internalizing behaviors including demanding attention, a need for perfection, being suspicious, having a hot temper, and finger sucking. Internalizing behaviors were reduced, with finger sucking and having a hot temper eliminated.

EXTERNALIZING BEHAVIORS

The remaining three questions checked whining, vandalism, and hanging with other troubled children. Each of those behaviors was reduced with whining eliminated as per the parent and teacher ratings, in the post test. The individual and group therapeutic sessions were more than helpful in assisting participants in changing their behavior.

LIMITATIONS OF THE STUDY

Among the limitations of this study are the implicit biases of the measures that were not developed for this purpose in the Child Behavior Checklist. Twenty of the questions that assess aggression and disruptive impulses were chosen and reviewed. To this end, the identified questions may not reflect actual aggression or disruptive impulses. The study is one that shows correlation or relationship and is not causal, so the assertion that the intervention caused good results, excluding other factors over which we have no control like family trauma and community empowerment are inappropriate. The African Cultural Arts program was a function of historic and contemporary resources. It is possible that necessary resources might not be available in some environments. The author looks forward to conducting this work with a larger group of participants, under different circumstances to see if the same results would be evident.

At the end of the academic year all but two of the participants left the more restricted M.A. program and were promoted to the next grade entering in class support or resource programs which included general education classes. While the participants began the year in the more restrictive in-district, out of district program 30 of the students were enrolled in the lesser restrictive in class support or resource programs. One participant continued in the M. A program and the other participant transferred to a school out of the state. It is not known if that participant continued in a less restrictive program.

Another limitation of this study is that only 32 fifth graders participated. A larger sample might show that the more students did not benefit from the ACA intervention and natural maturation factors. It is the author's hope that a larger sample that includes both girls and boys, classified as "emotionally disturbed" would show similar results. Additional studies need to be conducted to examine this idea. Generalizations about the study's effects are limited. Children who are not classified might respond differently to the group drumming intervention, since it was structured with emotionally challenged children in mind. The ACA program was structured to provide interim encouragement and reward for even the smallest changes in behavior that might lead to a reduction in aggressive behaviors and disruptive impulses. Since the participants were very familiar with not meeting expectations of parents and teachers, the program was flexible. In some instances, participants elected to drum together inside instead of taking recess in play areas outside with their general education peers. In addition, when participants wore traditional African dress to school they were acknowledged. These and other encouragements helped to reinforce the positive changes participants had begun to make.

The raters of the students, pre and post, were parents and teachers, grouped together. It is very possible that these raters were biased and may have had a personal investment in seeing the program work well. These raters were the only source of data. Future studies should separate these rater groups, to see differences more clearly. Other sources of data may have provided good evidence of the effects of the program. It is not clear if the drumming portion of the intervention was the critical factor in the positive change or if other aspects of the ACA therapeutic program made the significant differences in behavior that the data showed. Future studies should include a control group that participated in counseling and other therapeutic supports like occupational therapy, physical therapy and speech, but did not have benefit of the drumming intervention.

IMPLICATIONS FOR SCHOOL PSYCHOLOGY

School psychologists often need readily accessible, low cost means for managing aggressive and disruptive students in school. Having several drums and facilitating a drumming group is possible, even if a skilled master drummer is not available. While rhythms from the Old Malian empire are ideal and meaningful, it is not necessary for specific rhythms to be taught in order to benefit from playing the drum. Good sounding, rhythms that students can play together can be created by the students themselves.

Drumming is fun and can be helpful for students who are not aggressive and do not display disruptive behaviors. School psychologists may be able to enjoy working with general education students who just want to drum, in addition to students who need to reduce aggressive behaviors as evidenced by the number of times the children had disciplinary sanctions imposed like suspension and detention. Even staff members might enjoy participating in a drumming group. This might assist in developing better relationships among staff members and students who otherwise might have difficulty getting along.

Group drumming can be performed in school and in the greater community. Performances of special education students that demonstrate their skill can help to foster positive impressions of those students. When families and friends of emotionally disturbed students have opportunities to be proud of the students these opportunities can encourage positive reinforcement of cooperative behavior.

Future Research

In an effort to extend and expand the research presented here, several kinds are appropriate. Both qualitative and quantitative studies could be designed and conducted to learn more about the reduction and elimination of aggressive behaviors and disruptive impulses among 10-year-old African American boys, classified as emotionally disturbed.

Longitudinal studies that look at the differences in parent and teacher ratings of African American boys in the four areas of behavior in regular intervals (perhaps every 4 years; at ages

10, 14 and 18) over significant periods of time could help to determine what reductions in behavior were sustained or increased. Physical aggression, social/emotional internalizing and externalizing behaviors could be adjusted for maturation levels into young adulthood. Instead of finger sucking, which might be noted at 10 years of age, participants could be asked about smoking and substance abuse at 14 and 18. This process could look at similar behaviors that would reflect the greater personal freedom of an adolescent as opposed to the rather controlled existence of a 10-year-old.

Qualitative research could provide insight about the maintaining of reductions of aggressive behaviors or their increase or decrease with maturity. Interviews of participants might help to understand why more exact reductions took place after 60 days.

Research that considers the reduction of aggressive behaviors and disruptive impulses and the impact on phonological processing would be very helpful. If reading ability could be improved as aggressive behaviors and disruptive impulses were reduced, this might provide more incentive for educational systems to adopt this method of behavior medication.

Finally, comparisons of the reductions in aggressive behaviors and disruptive impulses and other academic performances of participants would be helpful to explore. Noting if great self-control and good self - concept improved the academic habits and performances of participants might provide a stronger argument for including group drumming in schools for special needs and general education program children. Communities have for some time enjoyed artistic exploration, and educational programs that showcase the drum. On every continent drumming of some kind has amplified the human heart beat. The universality of the drum should be documented and connected in future research. Communities and schools would benefit from more cooperation, so that children can learn the benefits of group drumming early.

Artist-in-Residence positions should be a resource for each school system that wants to enhance the (resilience) skills for youth. Future research could prove the advantage of professional artists mentoring school children. Along with group drumming, cultural dance is a natural partner. While many boys and men were drummers in the old Malian empire, girls and women danced. Accompanying dance programs can be another great resource for school communities that is low cost and accessible. Researching the origin of the drum/dance relationship in primary cultures would be worthwhile.

SUMMARY

This study provided good evidence of the benefits of group drumming to reduce rage and make schooling a viable resource for children. Low cost and accessible, drumming can be free style or can follow ancient rhythms from almost every continent. In many central city communities, one can find an African dance class and skilled drummers who regularly play for that class. Japanese, Irish, Latin American cultures also use the drum in powerful ways.

The evidence of the transmission of the psychological effects of racial oppression represented in horrific evidence is the by- product of poverty. The purpose of this study was to teach children (both classified and general education students) in central city and surrounding community schools about their African history which is rich and about which they know little. The study participants were expected to be positively impacted by the group drumming intervention. That is, aggressive behaviors and disruptive impulses were expected to be reduced as a result of the weekly group drumming class in the context of the experimental, therapeutic in-district program. That was the case. With regard to the four areas of behavior examined — physical, social/emotional, internalizing and externalizing — all showed significant reductions as identified by parents and teachers via The Child Behavior Checklist for ages 6-18 Aggressive Behaviors and Disruptive Impulses.

This study provided good evidence of the benefits of group drumming to make schooling a viable resource for children. Low cost and accessible, drumming can be free style or can follow ancient rhythms from almost every continent. In many central city communities, one can find an African dance class and skilled drummers who regularly play for that class. Japanese, Irish, Latin American cultures also use the drum in powerful ways.

BIBLIOGRAPHY

Ani, Marimba (Richards, D.) (1994). Yorugu: An African-centered critique of European cultural thought and behavior. Trenton, NJ: Africa World Press.

Alvord, Mary K. & Grados, Judy J. (2005). Enhancing Resilience in Children: A Proactive Approach *Professional Psychology,* 36, 3, 238-245. doi:101037/0735-7028.36.3.238

Budge, E. A. Wallis. The Egyptian Book of the Dead: (The Papyrus of Ani) Egyptian Text Transliteration and Translation. New York: Dover Publications, 1967. Originally published in 1895 pp. 576-582.

Choi, Ae-Na, Soo Lee, Myeong & lee, Jung-Sook. (2008). Group Music Intervention Reduces Aggression and Improves Self-Esteem in Children with Highly Aggressive Behavior: A Pilot Controlled Trial. *Advance Access Publications 25.*Doi:10.1093/ecam/nem182

DeLucia-Waack, Janice L.; Gellman, Rebecca (2007). The Efficacy of Using Music in Children of Divorce Groups: Impact on Anxiety, Depression, and Irrational Beliefs About Divorce. *Group Dynamics: Theory, Research, and Practice 11,4,* p. 272-282. American Psychological Association. Doi: 10.1037/1089-2699.11.4.272.

Fenning, Pamela & Rose, Jennifer (2007). Overrepresentation of African American Students in Exclusionary Discipline The Role of School Policy. *Urban Education* November 2007 *vol. 42 no. 6 536-559.* doi: 10.1177/0042085907305039

Gray, A. E. L. (2011). Expressive art therapies: Working with survivors of torture. *Torture, 21*(1), 39-47.

Gold, Christian; Wigram, Tony & Voracek, Martin (2007). Predictors of change in music therapy with children and adolescents: The role of therapeutic techniques. *Psychology and Psychotherapy: Theory, Research and Practice 80,* 577-589. The British Psychological Society. Doi:10.1348/147608307x204396.

Hansen, Lauren. (2011). Evaluating a sensorimotor intervention in children who have experienced complex trauma: a pilot study [Electronic mailing list message]. Retrieved from http://digitalcommons.iwu.edu/psych_hon pro/151

Hanser, S. (2012). Music therapy- Based Mechanism for coping with stress and pain. *Journal of Urban Culture Research*, 98-107.

Ho, P., Tsao, J. C., Bloch, L., & Zeltzer, L. K. (2011). The impact of group drumming on social-emotional behavior in low-income children. *Evidence Based Complementary Alternative Medicine. 2011*: 250708.

Hussey, David L.; Laymanm Deborah (2003). Music Therapy with Emotionally Disturbed Children. *Vaccination News: Psychiatric Times 20, 6*

Jordans, M., Tol, W., Komproe, I., Susanty, D., Vallipuram, A., Ntamatumba, P., & Lasuba, A. (2012). Development of a multi-layered psychosocial care system for children in areas of political violence. *International Journal of Mental Health Systems, 4*(15), 1-12.

Kolko, David; Brent, David; Baugher, Marianne; Bridge, Jeffrey & Birmaher, Boris (2000). Cognitive and Family Therapies for Adolescent Depression: Treatment Specificity, Mediation, and Moderation *Journal of Consulting and Clinical Psychology 68,4,* p. 603-614. American Psychological Association. doi: 10:1037//0022-006X.68.4603.

Kamitsubo, K. (2012). "Yes, I can learn!" blending music instruction into music therapy. *Journal of Urban Culture Research*, 108-117.

Lev-Wiesel, R., Orkibi, H., & Federman, D. (2012). The Use of Creative Arts Therapies for Diagnostic and Therapeutic Purposes. *Journal of Urban Culture Research*, 16-25.

Monteiro, N., & Wall, D. J. (2011). African dance as healing modality throughout the diaspora:the use of ritual and movement to work through trauma. *The Journal of Pan African Studies, 4*(6), 234-252.

McKeever, C., Koroloff, N., & Faddis, C. (2006). The African American wellness Village in Portland, Oregon. *Preventing Chronic Disease, 3*(3).

Porges, S. W. (in press). *Symposium on Music Therapy& Trauma: Insights from the Polyvagal Theory.* New York: Satchnote Press.

Shields, Christina (2001). Music Education and Mentoring as Intervention for At-Risk Urban Adolescents: Their Self-Perceptions, Opinions and Attitudes. *Journal of Research in Music Education 49, 5* p. 273-286.

Skiba, Russell J. et al. (2002). The Color of Discipline: Sources of Racial and Gender Disproportionality in School Punishment. *The Urban Review 34(4),* 317-342.

Randall, Vernellia R. (1996). Slavery Segregation and Racism: Trusting the Health Care System Aint Always Easy: An African American Perspective on Bioethics HeinOnline -- 15 St. Louis U. Pub. L. Rev. 206 1995-1996

Robinson, Thomas N.; Killen, Joel D.; Kraemer, Helena C.; Wilson, Darrell M.;Matheson, Donna M.; Haskell, William L.; Pruitt, Leslie A.; Powell, Tiffany M.; Owens, Ayisha S.; Thompson Nikko S.; Flint-Moore, Natasha M.; Davis, GeAndra J.; Emig, Kara A.;Brown, Rebecca T.; Rochon, James; Green, Sarah & Varady, Ann. (2003) Dance and Reducing TelevisionViewing to Prevent Weight Gain in African American Girls:The Stanford GEMS Pilot Study. *Ethnicity and Disease 13,* Winter p.65-76.

Rutter, Michael Psychosocial resilience and protective mechanisms. American

Journal of Orthopsychiatry, Vol 57(3), Jul 1987, 316-331 http://dx.-doi.org/10.1111/j.1939- 0025.1987.tb03541.x

Vance, J. Eric; Bowen, Natasha; Fernandez, Gustavo; Thompson, Shealy (2002). Risk and Protective Factors as Predictors of Outcome in Adolescents with Psychiatric Disorder and Aggression. *Journal of the American Academy of Child & Adolescent Psychiatry 41,1,* p. 36-43 January.

Zwerling, Isreal The Creative Arts Therapies as "Real Therapies". Psychiatric Services, Vol 30(12) December 1979, 841-844 http://dx.doi.org/10.1176/ps.30.12.841

APPENDIX
INFORMED CONSENT FORM

<u>TITLE OF STUDY</u>

Improving Self-Concept of Urban Students

<u>TITLE OF STUDY IN LAY TERMS</u>

Can Drumming and Learning About Your History Make You Feel Better About Yourself and Make You Better At School Activities?

<u>PURPOSE</u>

The purpose of this research is to find out Can 30 minutes of African drumming each week, as a part of a comprehensive, therapeutic African Cultural Arts Program, reduce aggressive behaviors and disruptive impulses effectively enough, to encourage learning among children with psychiatric and social/emotional needs in group settings?

You and your child are being asked to be in this research study because your family depends upon the Urban Public Schools for a thorough and efficient education. If your child is not enrolled in the Urban Public Schools, you and your child can not be in this study.

INVESTIGATOR(S)

Principal Investigator: Dr. Yuma Tomes
Co-Investigator: Philadelphia College of Osteopathic Medicine
Department: School Psychology
Institution:
Department:
Address: 4190 City Avenue Philadelphia, PA 19131
Address:
Phone: 215-871-6946
Phone:
Responsible (Student) Investigator: Tammarra R. Jones

The treatment your child is being asked to volunteer for is part of a research project.

If you and your child have questions about this research, you and your child can call Dr. Yuma Tomes at (215) 871-6946.

If you and your child have any questions or problems during the study, you and your child can ask Dr. Tomes, who will be available during the entire study. If you want to know more about Dr. Tomes's background, or the rights of research subjects, you can call the PCOM Research Compliance Specialist at (215) 871-6782.

DESCRIPTION OF THE PROCEDURES

If your child decides to be in this study, your child will be asked to play an African drum, and explore information about the cultures who developed the instruments and the rhythmic patterns.

The study will take about 30 minutes for each session. There will be 3 session(s) over the course of 1 week, for a total of 5 hours of your child's time.

POTENTIAL BENEFITS

Among the potential benefits to participants are improved self-concept. We also expect improved academic performance and greater reliance on self- regulation. Learners may develop greater facility with social skills and become better able to interpret non-verbal messages. Your child may not benefit from being in this study. Other people in the future may benefit from what the researchers learn from the study.

RISKS AND DISCOMFORTS

Playing drums can cause discomfort or bruising to hands as they become adjusted to appropriate force playing drums. Usually adjustment occurs immediately.

ALTERNATIVES

The other choice is to not be in this study.

CONFIDENTIALITY

All information and records relating to your and your child's participation will be kept in a locked file. Only the researchers, members of the Institutional Review Board, and the U.S. Food and Drug Administration will be able to look at these records. If the results of this study are published, no names or other identifying information will be used.

REASONS YOUR CHILD MAY BE TAKEN OUT OF THE STUDY WITHOUT CONSENT

If health conditions occur that would make staying in the study possibly dangerous to your child, or if other conditions occur that would damage your child or your child's health, the researchers may take your child out of this study.

In addition, the entire study may be stopped if dangerous risks or side effects occur in other people.

NEW FINDINGS

If any new information develops that may affect your child's willingness to stay in this study, you and your child will be told about it.

INJURY

If your child is injured as a result of this research study, your child will be provided with immediate necessary care.

However, your child will not be reimbursed for care or receive other payment. PCOM will not be responsible for any of your child's bills, including any routine care under this program or reimbursement for any side effects that may occur as a result of this program.

If you and your child believe that your child has suffered injury or illness in the course of this research, you should notify the PCOM Research Compliance Specialist at (215) 871-6782. A review by a committee will be arranged to determine if the injury or illness is a result of your child's being in this research. You should also contact the PCOM Research Compliance Specialist if you and your child believe that you and your child have not been told enough about the risks, benefits, or other options, or that you and your child are being pressured to stay in this study against your wishes.

<u>VOLUNTARY PARTICIPATION</u>

You and your child may refuse to be in this study. You voluntarily consent to be in this study with the understanding of the known possible effects or hazards that might occur during this study. Not all the possible effects of the study are known.

You and your child may leave this study at any time.

If your child drops out of this study, there will be no penalty or loss of benefits to which you and your child are entitled.

I have had adequate time to read this form and I understand its contents. I have been given a copy for my personal records.

I agree to allow my child to be in this research study.

Signature of Parent :

____

Date: ______/______/______ Time: ________________AM/PM

Signature of Investigator or Designee (circle one):

____

Date: ______/______/______ Time: ________________AM/PM

Pre And Post Tests

DIRECTIONS: Please respond to the following questions about your child's or student's behavior within the last 3 months. Answer 0 for not true. Answer 1 for sometimes true. Answer 2 for very true.

1. Does your child/student act too young for his age?
    ______

2. Does your child/student cling to adults too much?
    ______

3. Is your child/student cruel to animals? ______

4. Does your child/student bully other children?
    ______

5. Does your child/student demand adult attention?
    ______

6. Does your child/student require perfection in his work? ______

7. Does your child/student fight with other children?
    ______

8. Does your child/student "hang" with troubled children? ______

9. Does your child/student lie to protect himself?

______

10. Has your child/student physically attacked others?

______

11. Does your child/student refuse to talk? ______

12. Does your child/student scream to communicate?

______

13. Does your child/student engage in clowning? ______

14. Is your child/student excessively suspicious? ______

15. Does your child/student use profanity? ______

16. Is your child/student "hot" tempered? ______

17. Does your child/student threaten people? ______

18. Does your child/student suck his fingers? ______

19. Does your child/student vandalize property? ______

20. Does your child/student whine to communicate?

______